WHAT WITH BEING STONE DEAF & EVERYTHING

DAVID HALLAMSHIRE

EBURY PRESS
LONDON

Thanks to Toni Canelli, Tom Heritage
and Pete Lawless without whose
help this book would still have
been written.

Published by Ebury Press
Division of The National Magazine Company Ltd
Colquhoun House
27–37 Broadwick Street
London W1V 1FR

First impression 1989

ISBN 0 85223 738 3

Edited by Miren Lopategui
Designed by Jerry Goldie
Illustrated by Martin Brown

Typeset by Textype Typesetters, Cambridge
Printed and bound in Great Britain at
The Bath Press, Avon

CONTENTS

HOW TO USE
THIS BOOK

Start at the beginning and read all the words one after the other until you come to the very end and then stop.

NOTE TO READERS: Throughout this book the reference to musicians is usually in the form of 'He.. His... Him' etc. Although a great many females are now taking part in rock and pop music, the male possessive has been used for two reasons:

1. It is more convenient than writing 'his/hers' all the time.
2. The author is a narrow minded sexist pig.

INTRODUCTION

The first experience you will have of being a musician is when your mother smacks you round the head.
The similarity being that this is *also* loud, physically disorientating and sends you deaf.

However, when you do become a real musician you will notice the difference immediately. It's a lot more fun than being smacked round the head and you can get drunk afterwards.

Not all musicians are rock musicians. Some people do make funny noises with violins in a thing called an orchestra. (An 'orchestra' is a large gathering of people who poke each other in the ear with sticks.) But for the purposes of this book I will deal with rock music and pop music, the subtle distinction being that 'rock music' is a loud aggressive exciting form of entertainment enjoyed by many people, whereas 'pop music' is garbage.

CHAPTER ONE

BECOMING A MUSICIAN

The first thing to do when wishing to become a musician is to find a second-hand shop to press your nose against. If it has the musical instrument of your choice in the window then all the better, but this is not essential. The main thing is that you once pressed your nose against the window of a second-hand shop, dreaming of your first guitar/drums/ saxophone, etc., so that you can tell people in interviews how you used to press your nose against the second-hand shop window dreaming of your first guitar/drums/ saxophone, etc. This is especially effective if you just happen to be surrounded by thousands of pounds worth of equipment whilst being interviewed. It will also give you some credibility to admit that although you are now a millionaire you were once skint, though this of course won't stop people wanting to kick your smug brains in.

Having found a second-hand shop to press your nose against, you should then save your pocket money week after week and run to the second-hand shop just to see if the guitar/drums/saxophone, etc., are still in the window. If your father bought your instrument for you then just lie. It makes a great story and the last thing the reporter will be interested in is the truth.

Having accumulated enough money you should now rush into the second-hand shop with 'GULLIBLE' written in

big letters on your forehead, and buy a musical instrument that nearly, but not quite, works. Buying a first instrument that actually works is against the laws of nature, so don't worry about it unduly as it will be some weeks before you realize there are bits missing.

(Saxophone players have spent many a happy hour learning to play a gas turbine stop valve and been none the wiser until they saw a picture of Charlie Parker. Who, incidentally, *could* play a gas turbine stop valve, though he probably didn't realize it at the time, as is illustrated by

7

the title of the famous Charlie Parker bootleg tapes, 'This Saxophone Sounds Like a Gas Turbine Stop Valve'.)

It should be noted that haggling with the person in the second-hand shop is pointless. It usually goes like this:,

How much is the guitar?

A hundred and fifteen.

I'll give you ninety.

It's a hundred and fifteen.

It's not worth more than a hundred.

It's a hundred and fifteen.

I'll give you a hundred and ten.

It's a hundred and fifteen.

A hundred and fifteen?

Yes.

O.K.

You should then rush home and make loud noises on your new instrument. It doesn't matter too much what these noises sound like as long as they are loud. And anyway, it will be quite a time before you realize that it's possible to tune the thing.

Very soon after this initial session you will probably hear a noise coming from the wall. Surprisingly enough, this is not a rock fan trying to break in and get your autograph, but is more likely to be the old bat next door who is upset about you making her hearing aid feed back. Just ignore it. After all, when you're famous she will be telling everyone she used to live next door to you.

WOMAN: He was ever such a nice boy. Always did errands for his Mother. I used to listen to him practising in the attic everyday.
REPORTER: Didn't his music ever disturb you?
WOMAN: Oh no. Never. He was ever such a nice boy.
REPORTER: So why did you shoot him?

8

Listening to records is always a good idea. So is eating, sleeping, saving money, marrying the right person, keeping your bowels open and thinking clean thoughts. However, as the main idea here is to talk about music then the listening of records is probably the most useful good idea of all the other good ideas. This is because listening to records will give you a pretty good idea of just how rubbishy you really are, and with a bit of luck you'll improve slightly. That is, of course, assuming that after listening to Clapton you don't smash up the record player with your 'second-hand Japanese copy of a copy of something that looks very similar to a Strat' guitar.

(It was this same type of musician's temper tantrum that caused Keith Moon to drive his Rolls Royce into his swimming pool, though why he thought his Rolls was a guitar and his swimming pool a record player can only be put down to what he was drinking. Or, as several party guests said at the time, 'Look at the colours, man.')

NOTE. •
A good way of overcoming intolerance from neighbours who don't like you practising, is to go next door, knock politely, and tell them to bollocks.

• •

CHAPTER TWO

MUSICAL INSTRUMENTS

All good musicians should have a full understanding of the different musical instruments in the band. This will ensure that they know where the funny noises are coming from and can bitch about the right person in the pub afterwards.

DRUMS

Drums are the name given to things that you hit. This should not be confused with the Roadie, which makes a different noise all together. They are played by shaking bits of your body at different times and hoping that if you place something in the way it will come out as a rhythm. Most drummers play the Drums with things called 'drumsticks', which are long pieces of wood used for throwing at the audience after the gig, and catapulting into the air off the Snare Drum during the exciting bits.

The other uses of the drumstick are for:
1. Twiddling in the fingers while someone is trying to talk to you.
2. Beating out a rhythm on a flight case while someone is trying to talk to you.
3. Beating out a rhythm on your legs while someone is

trying to talk to you.
4. Scratching various parts of your body while someone is trying to talk to you.
5. Pointing at things while talking to someone.

The Bass Drum is the most important part of the drum kit. This is because the drummer can spend hours messing around with it while everyone else is unloading the van.

The constant Thubum! Thubum! on the Bass Drum is the drummer's equivalent of 'Testing One two... One two.' It can get on your nerves after a while, but ignore it as the drummer gets little pleasure out of life, what with being stone deaf and everything. Let him have his fun.

The next most important part of the drum kit is the Snare Drum. This is in fact the least musical part of the drum kit but it makes more noise than the other bits, which is very important. Drums are, after all, for making lots of noise with. Ask any neighbour.

The Cymbals come next in the level of importance. The number of Cymbals a drummer has in his kit is inversely proportional to his talent as a drummer. This is because the Cymbals are used for hitting when you run out of things to do with the other bits. Therefore, the more cymbals you have the longer your incredibly boring solo can be, while actually sounding as if you are doing something different.

Really desperate drummers have a huge gong behind them. This is an Ossodit gong from Japan and is used when you have completely run out of ideas and think, 'Ossodit, I'll hit the gong.'

It is a sure sign that a drummer has come to the end of his incredibly long boring solo when he falls down dead, gets booed off the stage, or hits the gong.

Gongs are very versatile. You can hit them softly or very softly. Or you can hit them hard or very hard. It all sounds the same but who's listening anyway? And if you get really fed up with it you can use it as a wok.

NOTE. . . . .
Drums are round rather than square, so that there will be lots of nooks and crannies to put all the bits you forgot when packing the van.
. . . .

The first ever Drum was discovered by a primitive native who accidentally bashed a stick against a hollow tree. He liked the sound of it so much that he immediately grew his hair, donned a black T-shirt, found a pair of sticks and spent hours beating hell out of his mother's settee arms while everyone else was trying to watch the television. This strange way of acting has been copied by drummers ever since.

NOTE. . . . .
The first ever long boring drum solo to appear in the middle of rock music was performed by a drummer who hadn't realized the rest of the band had gone home. His name was Blind Willie Smith.

This should not be confused with the founder of Motorhead who was his brother, Deaf Willie Smith.
. . . .

Drums can actually be tuned. This can be quite a revelation to someone who has spent ten years just hitting the things and hoping something interesting comes out the other end. That is why, when you do a dramatic run round on a very expensive tuned kit it sounds like PHIM! DOO!

12

FEE! DOOBEDOO! as opposed to the cheaper kit which sounds like PHAM! PHAM! PHAM! PHAM-PHAM-PHAM!

GUITAR

A Guitar is a piece of wood with strings on it, used for picking up people of the opposite sex and making loud noises with. It is played by wearing tight trousers.

An Electric Guitar is supposed to be an extension of the male sexual organ, which is pretty weird. I've never seen one with strings, though I have seen people bashing them against microphone stands. Come to think of it... No. Maybe not.

The Electric Guitar should not be confused with a Bass Guitar which is used for giving you back ache and played by looking depressed. But then if you had to play the thing you'd be depressed too. The human brain can only cope with playing Fum Dum Dum Dum Dum Dum Dum Dum Fim Dim Dim Dim Fum Dum Dum Dum Fim Dim... for just so long.

The Acoustic Guitar is used for playing songs while everyone goes to the bar, or songs that have a political, ecological or feminist theme. In fact, anything really boring. That's why folk singers use them. This, of course, doesn't apply to Blues which can be played on anything if you are called Blind Lemon Willie Big Boy Slackgob Arkwright.

The Electric Guitar, on the other hand, is used for playing music that makes your ears bleed while jumping up and down in a tight group of sweating people. This should not be confused with jumping up and down inside a tight sweater, which is a lot more fun, depending on who's in it.

For the best effect an Electric Guitar should be played as if you are trying to strangle it. Or, even better, as if *it* is

trying to strangle *you*. You will see the rhythm guitarist doing this all the time, even though he's only got a few simple chords to play. This is because he feels intimidated by the lead guitarist who can play individual notes.

On the end of a guitar is a thing called a Machine Head. This is for the guitarist to play with between numbers and is nothing like a Motorhead, which is a type of brain disease whereby you think you are a car.

NOTE. . . . .
Famous quote from a member of Motorhead:
'Pardon'

. . . .

(A handy hint for guitarists is to look carefully at the strings
before playing.... There should be six. Also, if your Guitar

starts sounding very dead and losing the higher harmonics, you should remove the strings from the Guitar and boil it for ten minutes. This, however, is no real substitute for buying a new Guitar as boiling it will only work a few times.)

When you first start playing the Guitar you will find that the tips of the fingers on your left hand go very red and develop an excruciating pain. This can be caused by having the action too high, pressing too hard with your fingers, or just being a namby-pamby.

Do not worry. This pain will soon subside when you throw the Guitar away. It was this pain in the fingers that caused Pete Townsend to start smashing up his guitars on stage. Jimi Hendrix suffered from the same thing but he used to take out his frustration on the Guitar by biting bits out of it. Then again, as a lot of people later commented when explaining these actions, 'Look at the colours, man.'

As a beginner with an Acoustic Guitar you will also encounter the 'Plectrum Phenomenon'. This is the strange state of affairs where if you let go of the plectrum for a fraction of a second, it will leap inside your Guitar. No one knows why this happens, but it has been confirmed by many guitarists that inverting your Guitar and shaking it about will dislodge bus tickets, old biros, paper clips, and a 20-peseta coin. But no plectrum. However, when you've lost ten or more plectrums in the Guitar the chances of one falling out are now increased to 10,000 to 1 against. Logically this would mean that the best way to be sure of inverting your Guitar and getting a plectrum out is to put 10,000 plectrums in there in the first place.

This is thought to be linked to the 'Where's Me Soddin' Plectrum Phenomenon', which is where you put a plectrum down for a second and find that it has disappeared. Having a collection of several hundred plectrums spread about the house can sometimes overcome this problem, but not always.

Some people, having lost a thousand or so plectrums, then decide that finger-picking is a good idea, or would be if they had any fingernails. So they go out and buy a collection of plastic finger picks, which also leap inside the guitar at the least provocation. However, if you do find success with finger picks it is advised that you don't wear them all the time because when you come to pick your nose you will hook your brains out.

KEYBOARDS

T he term 'keyboards' covers all the different types of keyboard instrument. It's not worth listing them because a new one is invented every four seconds.

The Keyboard Player is included in the band because he is the one with all the money and without him there would be no PA. The Keyboards themselves are included so that the band can spend an extra hour dismantling things before they go home. This gives the sax and trombone players time to have sex in the dressing-room. Though not necessarily with each other.

The most popular way of playing a synthesizer is with one finger. This gives the player plenty of time to smile at the singer and jig about in a really sickening manner as if he is enjoying himself. It also helps enormously if the one-fingered synth player is a good-looking girl or boy, but the technique can be carried off successfully if you look like an out of work stockbroker on drugs.

The Electronic Keyboards also have a thing called a MIDI. This does a lot of interesting things but its main purpose is to give the Keyboard Player something to talk about.

Keyboards and MIDI are featured heavily on a programme called *Rock School* which is like *Blue Peter*,

17

only the presenters look more scared. They also make less mistakes which is very boring, but then so is *Blue Peter* now that John Noakes has stopped trying to kill himself every week. If you don't know who John Noakes was, he was… well, he was like… well… It doesn't really matter.

Rock School (with guest presenter, John Noakes):

JOHN: The good thing about the MIDI system is that we can still climb this fifteen thousand foot chimney and free fall parachute whilst playing the Polysynth II. A Polysynth II can be made quite easily using sticky back plastic. Here's one that I made this morn… AAaaaaaargh!

THE BASS PLAYER: *(looks into camera and blinks nervously as if just been shot)* Well, that now brings us to the new MIDI inter poly rhythmic syncopated cross hatch generator.

(He plays something physically impossible on bass and smiles as if just been shot again.) This can also be played in conjunction with keel hauling… John?

JOHN: Well, here I am being keel hauled whilst playing an inter poly rhythmic syncopated cross hatch generator… etc.

Electronic Keyboard Players tend to start off with a very simple notion of what is required to perform convincing music. A lot of them start off with a one-fingered technique. Then a few of them become interested and learn more complex keyboard skills. Then a few of them practise for ten years and get as good as Rick Wakeman. A few of these then go on to watch that bloke out of Weather Report and go home, set fire to every keyboard they possess and commit suicide.

18

SAXOPHONE

S axophones are becoming increasingly popular in bands that play pop music. This is because any jerk can play a Saxophone well enough for pop music. Ask any Kazoo player. This, of course, doesn't apply to jazz, but, then, what does?

A Saxophone is a sort of long tubular thing with lots of holes in it. It works by pressing your fingers on holes which immediately causes other holes to open. Unless you've pressed another key, in which case they'll all close. Simple, really.

The sound is made by blowing a reed, like a lollipop stick, against a mouthpiece and then sticking out your bottom jaw. It is this lollipop stick that Saxophone Players like to lick before playing, because the sudden tang of raspberry gets their mouth juices going.

Very near the lollipop stick at the top of the mouthpiece are two small screws on a device called the ligature. These are there so that the Sax Player has something to twiddle with between numbers. They are also very useful for looking at in a confused manner when you play a bum note. Saxophone players do this all the time. They call it 'harmonics'.

Saxophones belonging to professional players also have an occasional elastic band holding the keys down. This is supposed to give the impression that you are too busy touring to get it fixed. Whereas it's just because you're too lazy.

N O T E. . . . .
Saxophones come in two types:
1. *Selmer Mk6.*
2. *Others.*
. . . .

In order to keep a Saxophone in good working order after it has been played, it should be thoroughly cleaned through with a long woolly flue brush. The reed should be removed from the mouthpiece and wiped, and the mouthpiece should be wiped through with a light duster. If you watch professional Saxophone Players, you will see them doing this approximately never.

Charlie Parker's method of looking after his Saxophone was to fling it off the stage and then fall down. This is only slightly different to the method of a little-known Sax Player called Cool Drool, who used to conclude his evening's playing by letting the sax fall down and then flinging himself off stage. His last ever performance was conducted in complete silence when he forgot to bring his sax with him and thought the audience wouldn't notice.

The band let their feelings be known about this slip in professionalism by dropping him off on the M6, at 70 m.p.h., tied in a brown sack.

NOTE . . . .

The modern saxophone was invented by Adolf Sax. This should not be confused with the inventor of the trumpet, who was Adolf Trump.

. . . .

TRUMPET

A Trumpet is quite straightforward. You spit down one end, twiddle your fingers up and down in the middle, and point the other end at someone in the front row.

When you get bored with filling the Trumpet full of spit, there's a little valve at the bottom which you can open between numbers and explode huge gobs all over the floor. This action should then be followed by moving the valves up and down very rapidly as if you know how to play the thing.

The first ever Trumpet was invented on the night a drunk fell out into the street and played a stolen coach horn. His neighbours complained, so he told them what they could do with it. They did. The result was the shape of the modern Trumpet.

Valves were only added later when someone accidentally bought a gas turbine stop valve and fitted it to a trumpet. To everyone's astonishment the new modern Trumpet was capable of playing really nauseating Christmas songs and the theme from *The Deer Hunter*. This, of course, still goes on today.

Trumpets have things called mutes. This is a sort of traffic cone that is rammed up the trumpet to give the rest of the band a break in the quiet bits of the song. Trumpet players don't like using a mute because it makes them want to blow harder and their ears bleed.

Most Trumpets point in a straight line from the Trumpet Player to the audience, unless you fall off the stage (see Dizzy Gillespie).

One of the most famous Trumpet Players was called Louis Armstrong. He specialized in playing the Trumpet and then singing as if he had a dustbin lid lodged in his throat. His nickname was Satchmo, which is Latin for 'dustbin lid lodged in throat'. He is also famous for the song with the line, 'And I think to myself, what a wonderful world.' The popularity of this song caused the biggest outbreak of laryngitis ever recorded in history.

TROMBONE

A Trombone is another instrument used in the 'brass' section. Which, incidentally, is called the 'brass' section because it gets paid the most for doing the least.

A Trombone is used for poking the keyboard player in the back of the head and making loud rasping noises with. It would have gone into obscurity and never been seen again if 76 of them hadn't appeared in a big parade. Which just goes to show that anything will catch on, no matter how awful, if you have enough of them. Take violins, for instance.

Trombone Players like spraying strange liquids on to the Trombone slide and then moving it up and down very quickly. This doesn't achieve any mechanical efficiency, but it gives the Trombone Player something to do when he isn't making fun of the singer.

A popular piece of music for several Trombones is called 'Holiday for Trombones', which is pretty stupid as the only people who have to play it are the Trombonists, whereas everyone else has gone on holiday.

The most well known Trombone Player in the country is George Chisholm. Which makes you think.

TAMBOURINE

This is not a musical instrument. There is absolutely nothing, at all, what-so-ever, musical about a tambourine. This is why it is safe in the hands of the lead singer, who thinks there is.

CHAPTER THREE

JOINING THE BAND

After a whole three weeks practising in your room you should be about ready to join a band. Worrying about the fact that you can't play is a defeatist attitude, and anyway, just play it loud. It'll still sound horrible, but it's a lot more fun.

There are two main ways of getting into a band. The first and easiest way is to hang around pubs where musicians go. Then as soon as someone leaves a band you make your presence known by just happening to have your guitar with you and breaking into song. Oddly enough, you will find that although you are playing acoustic guitar you will be backed by drums, bass, brass section and orchestra. (I don't know why this is, but it always worked for Elvis Presley.) Then a man called Sam will come from behind the bar and say, 'You've got the job, kid.'

If this doesn't work, the other method of getting into a band is to answer the many adverts stuck on the notice board in your local music shop. (Don't go for the French lessons. They're terrific but you don't get paid.)

They will say such things as:

'Drummer wanted for progressive heavy metal reggae rock dance band. No time wasters.'

The actual notices themselves can be quite an education

when you realize the difference between what they say and what they actually mean.

1. 'POSSIBLE RECORDING DEAL.'
   (The band have just met a man with a cigar.)
2. 'WORKING BAND.'
   (Done two gigs and broken even.)
3. 'SINGER REQUIRES BACKING GROUP.'
   (Some clod of a singer is 'pursuing a solo career' because the band booted him out.)
4. 'NO TIME WASTERS.'
   (Must have lots of money and a P.A.)

Some of these notices are actually quite stupid. Like 'Must be able to read'. You wouldn't be reading the notice if you couldn't read. And then, 'Band scores'. Is this a statement or just boasting?

If you can't play progressive heavy metal reggae rock dance music, then go along to the audition anyway. The chances are they can't either.

THE AUDITION

T he Audition is a meeting of people, usually held somewhere cold and damp so that you don't enjoy it. The people holding the Audition are called the 'band'.

25

They will make a big thing about the fact that they are the 'band', by dressing in something really stupid, so that no matter what you are wearing, you look a prat.

If you turn up in a suit they will be wearing bondage wellingtons and shaved heads. If you turn up with 'Death' tattoed across your head, they will be dressed for tea with the Queen.

In fact, this is of such great psychological importance that if you turn up wearing the 'right' clothes you will immediately get the job without even playing a note, as it is assumed that anyone who dresses as stupidly as the band do must be the right person.

Even worse than the problem of what to wear is the part where you have to play. This is usually set in motion by two things, both designed to make you look stupid. The first is where they say, 'Play something', and you have only ever played along to records so don't actually know a solo. And the second is where they play a tape of their excruciating song for 30 seconds and think that by some unseen telepathic power, you can play the whole thing right through. This is very hard to do. Especially when they come to the bit that they forgot to tell you about that changes to 13/7 for two bars and then back to 5/9 because the musically illiterate idiot who wrote it doesn't know what he is doing.

It's round about now that they start arguing among themselves and you realize that the real leader of the band isn't the singer after all, but the guitarist. This is because he's the only one in the room who appears to know what he's talking about. They will all then launch into a deep discussion as to what the real rhythm should be and with any luck you will be forgotten. This means you have got the job.

The other way of getting the job is when one of them cocks his trilby to the back of his head and says, 'OK. Let's hear you, kid.' You should then play a song on acoustic guitar, backed by drums, bass, brass section and orchestra even though no one else is playing. This is another method that Elvis Presley used.

One of them will then come up to you and place his hand on your shoulder as he says, 'You start tomorrow, kid.' It will help enormously at this point if you can get a dumb blond to hook an arm through yours and look up at you adoringly. Preferably a dumb blond of the opposite sex.

There is then an adjournment to the pub where everyone tries to pretend they like you, even though you've only just met them. They will then ask you tentative questions to determine if you are a berk or not, and you should then ask them carefully phrased questions to see if they've got a hope in hell of earning any money before the year 2020.

You can then go home and tell your mother/girlfriend/ boyfriend/sponsor/bank manager, that you have joined a band and are going to be famous. To which there will be absolutely no response. But then what do they know anyway?

Previously Unknown Scenes From History: No 1

ELVIS: I've joined a band, Mom, and I'm going to be the most famous Rock and Roll singer who ever lived.

MOTHER: Eat nicely now.

CHAPTER FOUR

THE REHEARSAL ROOM

The Rehearsal Room is usually some God-forsaken pit of a hole in the basement or upper floor of a nearly disused factory. They are usually very very cold. Even in summer. This is so that you are left in no doubt that you are a struggling musician.

Rehearsal Rooms always smell of old sweat, damp carpets, and rubber. This is quite confusing at first until you realize that the smell is coming from the Roadie.

A really top-quality Rehearsal Room will have nearly, but not quite, enough light. There will also be lots of old beer cans, take-away food trays and enough tab ends on the floor to roll 80 Woodbines. Which is in fact what the Roadie does while everyone is playing.

The Roadie, by the way, is usually a friend of the band who has nowhere to go in an evening so gets conned into humping gear around just so that he can keep warm. After a few months he will forget that he doesn't have to do it, but will do it anyway.

It is also preferable if the Rehearsal Room is in the area of the city with the highest crime rate. This gives you ample excuse to fit the standard eight padlocks, bulletproof steel sheeting, anti-tank radar and nuclear warhead to the Rehearsal Room door. It doesn't, however, stop the thieves getting in the window, but it does give the impression to an outsider that your equipment is worth ten times more than it actually is. Which is probably why it got nicked in the first place.

The other interesting thing about a Rehearsal Room is that it is never easy to get equipment in or out of. This is because you have to go down or up some steps which are exactly half an inch smaller than your biggest speaker cabinet. (Or were, until you smashed your way up the stairs when you first moved in and enlarged the corners a little.)

To set out your Rehearsal Room properly you should ensure that there are lots of things to trip over. Just laying a few coiled leads here and there is not quite enough. For the really professional effect you should have a piece of carpet that keeps getting rucked up so that you nearly brain yourself on the drum kit every time you move a foot. This is especially effective if there are strange bumps, jagged water pipes and holes in the floor.

NOTE . . . .

Do not be alarmed if you should find a large lump under the moth eaten carpet and it keeps moving. This is the Roadie looking for things to eat.

If you find a large lump under the moth eaten carpet and the Roadie is visible, then be alarmed. This is either a rat, or the Drug Squad.

. . . .

One of the biggest problems with a Rehearsal Room (apart from nearly freezing to death) is the lack of a mains socket. This is usually overcome by having an extension lead plugged into the single 13-amp socket, which then has two extension leads plugged into it, which then has four extension leads plugged into them. This comes to about 184 amps. Don't worry about this. When all the wires start melting it will warm the place up a bit.

Posters are also an essential part of the Rehearsal Room. They can be used to cover the walls in an array of musical tastes, showing any guests who might drop by just what a hip groovy happening heavy today type of band you really are. Even when the music you actually play sounds like a duck with rabies and has as much street cred as a Marks & Spencer anorak.

For the fully professional effect there should also be an electric fire or fan heater somewhere. It doesn't matter which one you choose, as long as it is absolutely useless.

REHEARSING

'Rehearsing' is a name given to the occasion when the band gets together every week to argue. At least that seems to be the general idea.

It is always best to get to the rehearsal room quite early. This ensures that you are included in all the

30

bitching before the others get there and you are less likely to get thrown out of the band.

A proper rehearsal starts with all the band standing around saying how cold it is and waiting for the singer to turn up. This conversation is usually accompanied by the drummer who keeps going Thubum! Thubum! on the bass drum for no reason at all. That is, when he's not bashing

out a rhythm on a flight case while you're trying to talk to him.

NOTE. •
Drummers like to do Paradiddles. This should not be confused with a Para-piddle, which is when you wet yourself leaping from an aeroplane.
• •

The band will then get vaguely ready and the guitarist will play the same stupid riff that he plays every single week without fail, because it was the first thing he ever copied from a record and got right and still thinks everyone is impressed even though they've heard it a thousand times.

The bass guitarist will then put his bass guitar round his neck and look depressed. He will then play either nothing at all, or the only bit of slap bass technique he knows. Then he will carry on looking depressed and wait for everyone else to get ready.

The drummer by this time will have increased the frequency of the Thubum! Thubum! and may even hit the snare drum just for fun. Drummers very rarely play a show-off piece when they warm up, because nine times out of ten they get it wrong. Therefore, they usually save the show-off bits for the actual song, because when it goes wrong nobody is listening anyway.

It is about now that the lead singer turns up and brings everyone to a grinding halt by discussing something he read in *NME*. Then the drummer will get bored and go Thubum! and everyone will remember they are supposed to be rehearsing.

About an hour and three quarters after this, everyone will have finally agreed on what they are going to play and launch into the song. Three bars into this, either the sax player or the singer's girlfriend will turn up and bring everything to a grinding halt again.

Then, when the conversation starts fading, the guitarist will do his composer routine. It varies from week to week and band to band, but the essential elements are usually the same. The 'composer routine' is where the guitarist says, 'I've been thinking about this idea. What do you think?' He then plays three bars and stops. Everyone looks at him. He looks at everyone. Then he says, 'Well I thought if you could add a bass line or something...' Everyone looks at him. He looks at everyone. Then the drummer goes Thubum! and everyone spontaneously plays the only song they all know all the way through. Then everyone gets bored and goes to the nearest pub which is terrible but only across the road from the rehearsal room.

NOTE. . . . .

Attending the meeting in the pub after rehearsals is essential. The people who do not attend will be bitched about and thrown out of the band.

. . . .

THE BAND NAME

The Band Name is very important. This is because it gives everyone something to talk about for weeks on end when they meet in the pub after the rehearsal.

It should always be remembered that once you have chosen your name, *NME*, Radio 1, and *Smash Hits* will immediately abbreviate it so that it makes them sound as if they know you so well they had lunch with you last week – for example, Duran, B.A.D., Purple, Zeppelin, Fuzzbox, Curiosity, etc.

This is always worth remembering when choosing a name like The Impish Titantic Survivors (TITS) or The Fartown Stompers (The Farts).

Successful Band Names
1. Genesis.
2. U2.
3. The Who.
4. Dire Straits.

Unsuccessful Band Names
1. I'm So Fluffy.
2. Poo Bear and The Tiggers.
3. My Granny Eats Dead Goats and We're Going to Use It.
4. Freddy and His Erotic Dancing Sheep Farm.
5. The Gary Glitter Reincarnation Come Back Tour.

It is always enlightening to read the different names of bands which are sprayed on the cabs and PA stacks of a newly formed band. To an onlooker these would seem to be the names of the bands that the members originally belonged to, whereas it's actually the name of the band they stole the equipment from.

Great care should be taken when choosing a Band Name because of the presumption made about the type of music you play. A band called the Society Four are very likely to find themselves booked to play an afternoon tea dance and could be quite disappointing to the punters if they turn out to be a punk band. The band will have a riot, but the audience might not like it.

A good example of this is The Sisters of Mercy, who still haven't got over the incident at the vicarage garden party. But, then, neither has the vicar, who was last seen wearing a black leather jacket and shades and gobbing at a lady from the Women's Institute.

CHAPTER FIVE

BAND MEMBERS

O nce you have been in a band for a few weeks you will begin to recognize the main characteristics of each member. Bands vary a great deal but some things will always remain the same.

THE MALE LEAD SINGER

T his is the person for whom the whole band exists. Or so he thinks. The fact that it was the guitarist who put the band together, wrote the songs, hired the rehearsal room and booked the gigs, will not prevent the singer from calling it *his* band.

The Male Lead Singer will always be the one who insists on standing in front of everyone during the photo session, and giving interviews even though he doesn't know what he is talking about. And, strangely enough, the more he believes he is the centre of attraction the more he will talk as if he is giving an interview, even when doing something quite simple, like standing at the bar. e.g.:

PERSON: Do you fancy a pint?

SINGER: Well in the early days of course, I used to drink pints. I mean, that was all we had. We used to walk into these places, like bars and order pints of bitter all the time.

PERSON: Look! Are you listening to me? Do you want a pint or not?
SINGER: It was Chris who came across this idea of having just a half pint of bitter and adding a half of cider during the mix. Like mixing them down together. I remember we thought it was really a revolutionary thing to do, but we were only kids then.
PERSON: Do you want a pint or not!!
SINGER: That's why the new album is called Snakebite… Named after Steve's girlfriend. etc.

This sort of behaviour is quite common and shouldn't be allowed to worry you. Anyone who makes a fool of themselves as much as the singer does, should be allowed these little eccentricities.

The Male Lead Singer is always neurotic about the sound of his voice. Which, when you hear it without reverb, is quite understandable.

NOTE. . . . .
Roadies do not like lead singers. This is because singers tend to keep pointing the microphone at the PA and then blaming the Roadie for the feedback. This can be quite irritating for the Roadie when he has just had his eardrums imploded.

. . . .

Lead Singers have very little dress sense. This ensures that they always wear something really stupid and through no fault of their own become leaders of fashion. This is because the people who copy the dress of the Lead Singer are gullible morons who have no dress sense either. And it doesn't even require a record deal or any fame at all to make the Male Lead Singer believe he is likely to appear on the front of *Time Out* any day now. Even if he is penniless, blind drunk, and being sick, he will make sure the policeman arresting him only sees his good side.

This constant vanity is most evident when you point to a shop window and ask the Male Lead Singer what he sees. His reply will invariably be, 'Me.'

Should the band actually get a record deal, or get even the slightest hint of 'possibly' appearing on the *Bob Star Says Your New Face Has Opportunities Show*, then things really take off. Even though the Male Lead Singer has never been seen to smoke he will suddenly be sporting a packet of Black Russian cigarettes or those puffy little cigarillos with the plastic holders. This will then be followed by him doing something incredibly stupid with his hair and maybe even buying a strange coat that looks like it should belong to a Mississippi gambler. That is assuming that he hasn't already bought a stupid hat first.

Either way, he looks pretty silly, but it will be because of this that he becomes a leader of fashion and maybe even as famous as he always thought he was.

NOTE. •
An 'individual' is someone who 'wants to be different' by going to concerts and hanging around with two thousand people dressed exactly the same.

• •

Previously Unknown Scenes From History: No 2

CLIFF RICHARD'S MUM: You're not going out looking like *that* are you?

THE FEMALE LEAD SINGER

All the above applies to the Female Lead Singer, except for the feedback. Female Lead Singers do not blame the Roadie for the feedback, because they think it is part of the song anyway.

The Female Lead Singer's job is to spend all night looking like she'll have sex with anyone and then spending all night making sure that she doesn't.

All Female Singers are called Carol, Julie, Susan or Sharon. Those that aren't, are lying.

A lot of Female Singers usually insist on having the changing room all to themselves whilst the rest of the band change in the toilets. This, they insist, is because they are ladies. This comment in itself can lead to a whole evening's entertainment.

NOTE. . . . .

The Female Singer doesn't like the Male Singer
because he can't sing. He doesn't like her for
exactly the same reason.

. . . .

Most Female Singers have spent a lot of time in male
company. This gives them a great sense of self-worth and
independence. It is this that gives them a tendency
towards feminism. Feminist singers are rather tricky to
get on with as they tend to spend a great deal of time
walking around with their chest hanging out while
wearing black stockings and a mini skirt, then accusing
every male of being sexist. Which they are.

Having done this, and become successful, they then
complain that no one takes them seriously. Which is true.

Previously Unknown Moments in History: No 3

PERSON: How are you feeling?

MORRISSEY: Fine, thanks.

THE LEAD GUITARIST

The Lead Guitarist is the one who gets to play the
loudest solos. Lead Guitarists are under the
impression that the more they look in pain, the better the
solo. If a guitar was as hard to play as a Lead Guitarist
makes it look, no one would take it up in the first place.

The Lead Guitarist is the one that the little girls idolize
when they get bored of idolizing the Lead Singer. This is
because he wears tighter trousers than the Lead Singer,
which might explain why he looks in pain all the time.

In a newly formed band, it is the Lead Guitarist's job to get very ratty and moan at everyone before the gig starts. This can sometimes be done by the Singer, but the Guitarist does it so much better, because no one listens to the Singer anyway. The things that he should moan about are the lack of microphones, the lack of fold back monitors and the lack of an audience. Moaning about the bar not being open is usually left to the Trumpet Player and the Roadie.

After the gig the Guitarist's job is to get ratty because all the little girls are talking to the Singer, when it was the Guitarist who put the band together, booked the rehearsal room, and wrote all the songs. This is quite common, as is the Guitarist's habit of playing power chords when you are trying to tune up.

Another thing that the Guitarist seems to spend a lot of time doing is fiddling with leads. Especially the ones that go PHAM!!! BHURMMMM! NNNNNnnnnn!! nnnnnnnnnnnn! He will then look down at his guitar and then across to his amp and tap the lead. As he taps it there will be a strange noise as if all the cones on every speaker have suddenly snapped out as far as they can go. This is usually what is happening. There will then be a loud PHAM!!! BHUrmmm mm! and everything will be back to normal.

All this usually precedes the ritual of grabbing a lead and flicking it several times, then spiralling it in a circle as if he is about to lasso a buffalo, or trying to tie a one-handed reef knot.

THE RHYTHM GUITARIST

T he Rhythm Guitarist gets to play all the bits you can't hear unless you really listen for them. This is because he can't play solos, even though he wears tight trousers.

A lot of Rhythm Guitarists can play bass guitar. Which

explains a lot. They also spend a great deal of time learning techniques that make them look like they're doing something really complicated when they're doing something quite simple. These techniques include:

1. Playing the strings near the bridge.
2. Playing the strings up the neck.
3. Playing the strings in the middle.

As you can see, they get pretty frustrated with this set-up. It is because of this that the Rhythm Guitarist does such things as having ridiculous haircuts and dancing like a demented lunatic. It's the only way he can attract attention to himself.

The Rhythm Guitarist is very friendly with the Lead Guitarist. This is because he is secretly learning as much as he can from the Lead Guitarist in the hope that some day he'll drop dead and leave the job vacant.

THE BASS GUITARIST

The Bass Guitarist tends to spend most of his time looking like he isn't enjoying himself. The main reason for this is because the female singer won't sleep with him. But he also finds it a bit depressing that he can't leap about the stage playing the bass guitar as if he is trying to strangle it, like the Lead Guitarist does. This has been tried, but somehow it just doesn't come off.

To overcome this a new technique was developed. This involves knocking seven bells out of your right hand by slapping it against the strings. This tends to make you like you've got pins and needles in your hand and are trying to get the blood back into it, but it's a lot more exciting than plucking the strings normally. Unfortunately, it also makes your thumb drop off. This is why a lot of Bass

Guitarists have their thumb stuck back on with a piece of gaffer tape.

Bass Guitarists do tend to have a dry sense of humour. Their humour is so dry that sometimes even *they* don't know they've said something funny. This, however, doesn't stop everyone from falling about laughing.

Bass Guitarists also spend a lot of time looking at the drummer. This can be because they are trying to keep time together, but it's usually because the Bass Player is trying to work out what the hell the drummer is doing.

N O T E . •

When a Bass Guitarist smiles, it is usually because he has worked out what the hell the drummer is doing.

When a drummer smiles it is usually because he's got a drumstick caught in a funny place, or he's cocked up the Bass Guitarist again.

• •

THE DRUMMER

The Drummer is someone who has found a commercial outlet for Parkinson's disease. If you see a Drummer standing still it is because he is dead.

Drummers find it physically impossible to remain still for more than a tenth of a second. And even then they regard that tenth of a second as an off beat. They are easily identifiable, no matter what they are doing. Drummers are the only people who can tap their fingers in boredom in 5/7 time, whilst playing a non-existent high hat with their foot.

Drummers also tend to get into fights when they 'weren't doing anything'. What the Drummer was unaware

42

of when he 'weren't doing anything' is that sitting next to
someone who is tapping the table, floor, seat, ceiling,
window-sill, floor, walls, tables, chairs, with their foot
every fraction of a second, can drive people insane.

(The Chinese actually developed a torture whereby
they strapped someone to a seat on a train from Leeds to
London and sat a Drummer next to him all the way. The
victim managed to escape and throw himself from the
train just outside Bedford. When asked about it some
years late on *Panorama*, the Drummer said, 'I weren't
doing anything'.)

NOTE. . . . .
*NEVER! take a Drummer to a Chinese
Restaurant. As soon as he gets hold of the
chopsticks there will be prawn balls
everywhere.*
. . . .

The Drummer is one of the few people in the band who
gets on with the Roadie. This is because they both like the
same things; eating and hitting things. And what with them
both being stone deaf and everything...

The Drummer's main occupation, when he isn't going
Thubum! on the bass drum, or bashing out a rhythm on a
flight case while someone is trying to talk to him, is
listening to other Drummers going Thumbum! and
bashing out a rhythm on a snare drum. This is one of the
few reasons why they are deaf. When they are doing
neither of these things they are eating.

NOTE. . . . .
Drummers hate audiences that clap on the on
beat. But, then, doesn't everybody?
. . . .

Drummers tend to have a large appetite. This is because they spend all day moving around and burning up energy. A pedometer was recently fitted to a famous Drummer and it was found that he'd walked 20 miles in three hours. This would have been quite amazing in itself had he not been sitting down watching the television at the time.

N O T E . . . . .
*Drummers hate drum machines. This is because
they can play in 7/13 time without taking cocaine.*
. . . .

Most Drummers are more intelligent than they look. Which is just as well. When you think about it, they have to be intelligent to fasten all those fiddly bits together and make a drum kit. But sometimes they will stand still (nearly) and be completely perplexed by a simple thing like which way to turn a door handle. This is because they are trying to work out how Steve Gadd would do it before committing themselves.

THE KEYBOARD PLAYER

K eyboard Players come in two types. Those who can't play anything requiring a mental age above the age of three. And those who play like Chick Corea. For some strange reason the former get on *Top of The Pops* and the latter have to spend their life touring to make any money.

The Keyboard Player spends a great deal of time looking worried. This is quite understandable since the introduction of synthesizers to a band. With just one flick of a wrong switch, what was supposed to be a pleasant violin sound can come out as the fog horn of the *QE2*.

NOTE. •

It is impossible to make a pleasant violin sound on a synth. Violins can't do it, why should a synth?

• •

It is this uncertainty that causes really good synth players to spend all evening looking worried. They know their instrument inside out, and are fully aware that they can get

524 wrong sounds out of the thing. At least you know when you play a trumpet that the sound coming out of it isn't going to suddenly change to a helicopter. For the Keyboard Player this is not a certainty. This might be why a lot of Keyboard Players are called 'Stingray'. Because

anything can happen in the next half-hour.

When Keyboard Players aren't worried, they spend a lot of time reading about the latest synth to come on the market. This just makes them depressed, but it is best to leave them alone as they'll only start going on about MIDIs again.

N O T E . . . .

MIDI stands for Mindbendingly Intelligent Digital Interfacethingy.

. . . .

THE SAXOPHONE PLAYER

S axophone Players always look smug. Then again, if you could play one of those things competently, so would you.

When he isn't playing the saxophone or playing with the screws on the ligature the Sax Player tends to stare into the audience and nod to the music. What he is really doing is counting how much money has been taken on the door.

If the Sax Player is male, he tends to be the first person to pick up a girl after the gig. This isn't anything to do with him being any better-looking than the others. It's just that while everyone else is dismantling things he only has to slam his sax in a case and strut off. As do the Trumpet Player and the Trombone Players. However, the Sax Player has the edge on the other two because he doesn't have such a big pot belly.

Saxophone Players like doing 'harmonics'. This is where you make a squeak which is in tune with everything else you've played. It's quite tricky to do because you have to screw up your eyes and lean backwards as you point the sax at the ceiling. Trumpet Players don't do this because all the spit runs back down the tube.

A lot of Sax Players are called Zoot. And, strangely enough, they actually think this is a good thing to be called, whereas most people would be very upset if you implied they were a blue-faced felt hand puppet.

THE TRUMPET PLAYER

T he Trumpet Player spends most of his time exploding huge gobs of spit from the little valve at the end of the trumpet. But when he isn't doing that he's usually having a joke with the sax and trombone player about the lead singer.

Trumpet Players are the musical equivalent of the factory worker. They arrive, they play, they get paid, they go home. They rarely hang around to clear up the gear because they don't think it has anything to do with them.

NOTE. . . . .
A favourite word of the trumpet player is 'embouchure'. This is a French word that means 'spitting down a trumpet'.
. . . .

THE TROMBONE PLAYER

T rombone Players are usually loud and big. But not necessarily in that order. Novice Trombone Players who've only been playing for about 15 years still think it's funny to put the mouthpiece on their nose. Oddly enough, the Trumpet Player also thinks it's still funny. Which explains a lot.

Interesting things to do with a trombone:

1. Gum up the spit valve at the end of the slide and see how long it takes the Trombone Player to drown.
2. Ask the Trombone Player what the lowest note is on a trombone. He will then show you and the slide will fall off the end. Every single time.
3. Put a chamois leather on the end and clean the windows while practising.

THE BRASS SECTION

I t is mainly 'club' bands, or big name bands that have a Brass Section. This is because very few people can put up with them. They usually consist of the Sax Player, the Trumpet Player and the Trombone Player and spend most of their time fooling around at the back of the stage.

Because the Brass Section only have to do a few doo-wops every now and then, and the occasional ear-splitting solo, they tend to get a bit bored. It is this boredom that causes them to develop their very own stage act whilst the rest of the band are playing.

The stage act includes:
1. All wearing something silly.
2. Dancing like the Shadows.
3. Moving their instruments up and down in unison.
4. Trying to put people off when doing a solo.

Some really brilliant Brass Sections become almost a small act in themselves and may go so far as doing the soliloquy from *Hamlet* or firing the Trumpet Player from a cannon. Which is no bad thing.

THE ROADIE

T he good old Roadie. He is not actually a band member, but he's all part of the mess you'll find yourself in, so it's best to know a bit about him.

Roadies come in two types. The fat one that wears hipster jeans and T-shirt, and the thin one that wears hipster jeans and T-shirt. Both types smoke roll up cigarettes or in fact any cigarettes they can get their hands on and both types seem to get a psychological high from lifting heavy things.

The Fat Roadie will invariably wear a huge bundle of keys which are strapped to his belt. These keys don't actually fit anything but, boy, do they make him look important. It is also the weight of the keys that pull his trousers down so that you can see a chink of his bum every time he bends over. Which he does quite a lot.

The Roadie is a very important feature of the working band. It is his job to hump the gear, mix the sound, and make funny smells in the van on long journeys. Really big touring bands have a man for each of these jobs, but they all still make funny smells in the van on long journeys.

A lot of Roadies are responsible for sitting in front of the mixing desk getting drunk during a performance. Sometimes these people are called Sound Engineers, but that's just so that they will pick up more women than if they called themselves Roadies. They also like to twiddle with the knobs on the mixing desk whenever anyone is watching them. A lot of the time this is totally unnecessary but it makes them feel important. It also cocks up the sound.

Roadies like to talk about impedance, watts and RMS Output, which is fine if you know what they are talking about, but irritating if you don't. They may even sometimes talk about MIDIs but this is just so that the Keyboard Player will get friendly with them and give them cigarettes.

Roadies in touring bands also have a big sexual appetite, which they satisfy by having sex with ugly members of the audience in the back of the van. It can be assumed from a lot of these encounters that the Roadie is blind. When you see the Roadie after three days on the road and no change of T-shirt it can also be assumed that the people he ends up with are also blind.

This, however, won't prevent him giving the band a blow-by-blow account of last night's activities while he is making funny smells in the van on long journeys.

The Complete Roadie Kit

(Go on. Make a Roadie happy with this self-contained kit.)

1. A big bundle of keys.
2. Black Sabbath/Bruce Springsteen 1979 Tour T-shirt.
3. Six original anecdotes about working with other bands.
4. Four original anecdotes about sex in the van.
5. Two crates of strong German lager.
6. A bumper packet of Rizla.

Just send in four 'Complete Roadie' stickers and complete the following phrase, 'When I was in Hamburg...', in not more than 200 words.

The winning entry will get a FREE night out, throwing people off the stage at a David Bowie gig. (Back Stage Pass also supplied, so that you can clip it to your belt and look REALLY IMPORTANT!)

CHAPTER SIX

DIGS

The use of Digs by bands is becoming less frequent these days. This is because rather than spend months touring and getting very little money, sleep and satisfaction, it is more comfortable to make a demo tape and sell thousands of singles because you have been marketed by the Huge-Megastealing-Record-Company.

This lack of artistic struggle has even been transcended recently by people using sampling machines, which enable them to steal bits of other people's records in order to make a totally unique dance single. The fact that the dance single sounds like a mindless mess of stolen bits of other people's records doesn't prevent it from selling. Unfortunately. But I can dream.

This whole thing was summed up recently by a comment from one of the more articulate House Music fans who said, 'Er…'.

Anyway, for those bands who do actually go out into the world and play their instruments in front of real people, here is the low down on Digs.

Digs are where you stay when you can't get home after a gig. Digs are called 'digs' because most of them resemble holes in the ground. When you become rich and famous you will be able to stay in a 'hotel'. This is a type of Digs with more than one toilet. However, until that day comes along you will have to cope with 'digs'. These come in many forms and have a star rating all of their own.

ONE-STAR (★)

One-Star Digs are in fact, the back of the van. This is cold, damp, boring and horrible. Not unlike a bedsit. When you sleep in the van there is also nowhere to have a piss and so you have to revert to going out into the cold or using a milk bottle. Also like a bedsit.

It is also very inconvenient to have to share the van with the Roadie as there is nowhere to let out the funny smells, and as the Roadie lives on Vindaloo, the smells aren't very funny.

If you can survive the sub-zero temperatures and the funny smells coming from the Roadie, you will find that when you wake up it is raining. This is very odd, because you are in a van. However, when you look around you, you will find that the rain is coming from the roof of the van and falling in big blobs on to your sleeping bag. This is condensation. If the wet patch on your sleeping bag is not condensation then it is worth having a look to see what happened to the milk bottle someone used in the night.

Should you be lucky enough not to be sleeping in the van, it is always a good idea to wake up the members who are sleeping in the van by banging very hard on the door with the flat of your hand. This is very very funny. Or is, until the Roadie smashes your head in.

TWO-STAR (★ ★)

T he Two-Star Digs are a step up from sleeping in the back of the van. Not much. But better than nothing.

This is where you hire a single room in a Bed and Breakfast house and creep in one by one until all eight of the band are arranged on the floor in sleeping bags. This can be quite comfortable if you have left the Roadie in the van to make funny smells on his own. The only other problem being that seven people have to leave by the fire escape the next morning. In digs where more than one band are staying, the fire escape can resemble Oxford Street in the rush hour.

THREE-STAR (★ ★ ★)

T he Three-Star Digs come in the form of the Groupie. Or, rather, the Groupie's Flat. As in the expression, 'She's very accommodating.' This accounts for the reason why so many sane, good-looking musicians, end up with people that look as if they wrestle with bulls for a living. Anything is better than dossing in the van and it only takes a little prompting on your part to secure a bed for the night. The subtle approach is best. Something like: 'Are we going to your place or what?', will generally get the idea across.

The problem with this form of accommodation is that you:

1. Don't know when you are going to be beaten up by the lover who was supposed to be on night shift.
2. Don't get a lot of sleep.
3. Might catch something. (Cold, 'flu, etc.)

Remember, when staying at a Groupie's Flat it is always best to lie about everything. Give the Guitarist's name if you are the sax player. Give the wrong telephone number if you are asked for it and tell them you'll ring them when you get back to Sheffield/London etc. This may seem callous, but there will have been a lot of lying going on all night. ('I've never done this before,' etc.)

It also lessens the possibility of the lover coming to Sheffield/London and smashing your teeth down your throat.

FOUR-STAR (★ ★ ★ ★)

F our-Star Digs come in the form of a cheap commercial Bed and Breakfast house, where you might have to share a room with two people you've never met before. Do not worry about this. The Irish navvy and the lorry driver will think it's *you* that is the lower life form. Which in some cases might be perfectly true. And it's always better than sharing the van with the Roadie.

N O T E . . . .
Nylon sheets are always used in these places so that everyone will get caught up in them, get friction burns, get electrocuted and fall out of bed so many times that they will be up and ready for breakfast by six.
. . . .

It seems that people who snore are registered somehow and evenly distributed throughout the building so that if you do share a room it will be with a snorer. This must be to stop three snorers ending up in the same room and causing structural damage to the building.

Four-Star Digs always have a toilet on the landing somewhere, but you can never find it when it's dark because all the doors look the same and the bulb on the landing doesn't work.

FIVE-STAR (★ ★ ★ ★ ★)

I t should be remembered that Five-Star Digs = One-Star Hotel.

Five-Star digs are the Pro Digs. This is a grubby Bed and Breakfast place where people in the entertainment professions congregate. This arrangement allows a lot of people with ego problems to tell lies all night. 'We've been booked for Japan.' 'When I backed Paul Young', etc. However, the various characters you will meet can be quite interesting.

The girls who look like Strippers are Dancers, and the ones who look like Dancers are Strippers. However, the Strippers are easily identifiable as they can spit further. The people who look as if they haven't eaten for three days are the band, and the miserable git in the corner who looks half dead is the comedian.

Then there is always a 'Bobby Stallion', or someone with an equally macho name, who is 48, wears a wig, a gold sovereign ring, a white poly-cotton-satin-silk shirt (with frill down front), cuban-heeled white shoes and bri-nylon flared trousers and expects you to have heard of him because he was 'big in the sixties', as a singer.

He will tell you with great enthusiasm how he 'nearly' played the Palladium and is sometimes accompanied by his wife, 'Gloria Starling', who swears she is 27 and wears mini skirts even though she looks like Zelda out of the Terrahawks. They will then tell you about the time they had a BMW but have had to economize and now have a Cortina Escort which is just big enough to hold their couple of 2 × 12 cabs and WEM Copycat.

It is always worth listening to a Bobby Stallion life history at least once, then you can ignore the other hundred you will meet in your career.

One of the good things about a Pro Digs is that breakfast is served right up to 11.00 a.m. This is handy if you didn't get in until 2.00 a.m. anyway. It doesn't make the breakfast any better but at least you'll be awake enough to avoid eating the funny bits.

After breakfast you may be required to participate in a community exercise called 'Pushing the Van Out of the Car Park'. This usually follows immediately after the traditional 'Trying to Leave Without Paying'.

Previously Unknown Moments in History: No 4

SID VICIOUS: I'd really like to join the band, Johnny, but my heart's set on a nice job in the insurance business.

CHAPTER SEVEN

THE SOUND CHECK

The Sound Check is usually a farce. It's a little bit like Candy Floss. The idea is good but that's about it.

If you are actually lucky enough to get a Sound Check you will be instructed to arrive at the club at 4.00 p.m. This is just the management's little joke as you will not actually get a sound check until 7.30 p.m., or half an hour before the doors are opened to the public. Whichever is the most inconvenient. And even if you are allowed to do the Sound Check at some reasonable time you will still have to wait for the drummer and sound engineer to turn up because they're in a pub somewhere.

The first part of the Sound Check is done with the drummer. He sits himself down at the kit and plays a monotonous Thubum! Thubum! on the bass drum. Then the sound engineer/roadie says, 'Can you do that again?' and the drummer makes another Thubum! Thubum! sound and then suddenly flashes all round his kit because he's bored to death. Then he is instructed to play the tom-tom, which he does for about three seconds, then he flashes round the kit again because he is still bored to death. Then he plays the snare, and so it goes on. This usually means that the rest of the band only have two minutes to set up, tune up, and play the first verse of the opening song. Then everyone says 'To hell with it. That's near enough', and everyone retires to the bar.

No one actually knows why the Sound Check is done at a volume that verges on feedback. This is probably because the sound engineer/roadie is bored to death. And what, with being stone deaf and everything. . . .

When you come to actually play you will notice that the levels and sound balance are nearly but not quite exactly different to the way they were originally set up. This is because the management have adjusted the PA for their own purposes or the other band playing that night have followed you with their Sound Check and changed everything.

Shortly after the Sound Check you will find yourself in an activity called 'Sitting Around Being Really Bored'. This boredom can be alleviated by (1) Listening to the Roadie giving an account of his exploits in Hamburg; (2) Getting drunk; (3) Both.

Previously Unknown Scenes From History: No 5

SALESMAN: This is one of our finest guitars, sir.

HENDRIX: Oh. . . so *that's* a guitar.

CHAPTER EIGHT

THE WORKING MEN'S CLUB

The Working Men's Club is very common in Britain. It's pretty common at any time but it's most common in Britain. It is very likely that other countries have places where bands can die a thousand deaths but the Working Men's Club is the best.

The Working Men's Club is a whole world of its own. They have their own strange rituals and language, but there's nothing wrong with Working Men's Clubs. I was told to say that. (Thank you. No, £50 is fine.) Working Men's Clubs are wonderful and sophisticated and very nice places to spend a friendly evening. (Thank you. No, cash is OK.)

One of the many good points about the Northern Working Men's Club is the fact that the beer is always very good. This is because if bad beer is served in a Northern Working Men's Club the bar staff are taken out and hung up by their genitals from the nearest lamp post. This is where the expression, 'Now then, cock' comes from.

The original Working Men's Club was started by a lot of men who wanted somewhere to go after a hard day's work, so that they could play Bingo and win raffles after listening to someone singing copies of the latest chart sounds through a knackered PA. Or maybe that wasn't the original idea. But anyway:

THE DRESSING ROOM

The Dressing Room is a large cupboard next to the stage which contains old chairs, tables, a dead one-armed bandit, and the old Bingo machine. In fact, nothing worth stealing at all. It is here that the band can change into their stage gear before going out on stage to be totally ignored.

On the walls of the Dressing Room you will see various black and white publicity photographs. These are usually of acts that are dead, dying, or know Bobby Stallion. You

will also notice that they have been creatively scrawled on by other passing bands, so that everyone of them has a moustache and breasts or is involved in a creative sexual deviation. The funniest one is the photo of Bobby Stallion, aged 19, which he still hands out because that's what he thinks he looks like.

You may even occasionally come across a picture of Black Lace, but these are very rare as most of them were destroyed in the war.

When the band are in a state of undress there will be a light knock on the door. Opening it will reveal Tracy and Sharon (Darren Wayne and Kraig's sisters), who will giggle stupidly and ask for a signed photograph. This request will usually be granted by the lead singer who not only has an Adidas bag full of pictures of himself, but is stripped down to his leopard skin thong and thinks he look pretty good. The girls will then giggle a bit more and tell the band that they have 'seen it all before'. Which is probably true.

NOTE •
*At no time will you be able to find a coat hanger
in a Dressing Room. This is because they were
all melted down to help the war effort and have
never been replaced. (A war 'effort' is very
similar to a war 'thingy', which is like a 'doobrie'
only smaller.)*

• •

At about this point in the evening the female singer
will kick everyone out of the room, or someone will piss in
the sink. Or both. Either way it means it won't be long
before you go on stage, so now is the time to try and find
the trumpet player who will be round the bar somewhere
and wonder why you get so stroppy about him not helping
to move the PA. After all, it has nothing to do with him
because all he does is play the trumpet.

Everyone then gets a drink and huddles round a table
near the stage, whereby an old woman will lean
backwards and say 'You aren't loud are you?' (It's always
the woman who insists on sitting with her head in the bass
cab who says, 'You aren't loud are you?')

Then the drummer will drive everyone mad by
tapping his foot on the crossbar under the table so that
your beer goes flat even though he 'weren't doing
anything', and someone will be sent to try and find the
trumpet player who has gone looking for his lip.

NOTE •
*Trumpet players are constantly saying 'My lip's
gone', or 'Got to get my lip in'. Which is pretty
stupid no matter which way you look at it.*

• •

It's around the time that the trumpet player goes outside to bring his lip in that the Concert/Chairman/Secretary stands up in front of the stage and says something outrageous. This is always a laugh and worth listening to.

'Er... Er... Jeff is it on? Er... Right. Er... The winner of this week's raffle for a Beef Dinner is number... *(pushes glasses up nose)... is red... Red fifty-six... Purple, sorry... Is that red, Betty?... Purple fifty-six... Anyone? For a Beef Dinner... Fifty-six love... Purple... Anyone?... No?... Er... Er... Red then... Anyone with a red fifty-six... For a Beef Dinner.*

NOTE. •
A 'Beef Dinner' is a piece of cooked ham squashed between a raw pork chop and a bloody piece of beef and liver. This means one of the Committee is a butcher.

• •

If you are very unlucky there will then be a game of Bingo. If you have never been in a Working Men's Club during a game of Bingo, the following rules must be observed at all times.

1. Do not talk for any reason what-so-ever.
2. Do not laugh.
3. Do not breathe.
4. Do not stick your fingers up at the people giving you dirty looks just because you coughed.
5. Do not shout 'Bingo!', or 'House!'. This is hysterically funny at the time but it soon wears off when you realize 200 people want to kill you.

Around about now you should make your way back to the Dressing Room. If you can find the trumpet player it will help though he is most likely still looking for his lip.

Just when you have tuned everything up and anyone who can make noises with their instruments has made them, the Concert Committee Chairperson Secretary ('course, I was at Dunkirk you know), will burst into the Dressing Room hoping to find the female singer in a state of undress. He is very rarely that lucky, but will try week after week, just in case. He will then tell you to stop making a noise because the Tombola is on and will follow this with the famous ritual called the 'Three Twenties'. This is a dispute about the length of time the band should be on stage. It goes something like this:

> *CONCERT SECRETARY:* Can you do three twenties, love?
> *BAND:* We're doing two forties.
> *C/S:* Aaah... but can you do three twenties?
> *BAND:* We're booked for two forties.
> *C/S:* It'll mess up the Tombola.
> *BAND:* We only do two forties.
> *C/S:* You know it's a 'No pick-up' don't you?
> (Concert Secretary will then say 'Course, I'm seventy-eight, you know,' and leave)

NOTE. •
Concert Chairperson Secretaries always call Bingo by the name of 'Tombola'. They are both equally mindless so it doesn't really matter.

The phrase, 'You know it's a no pick-up?' is used as a parting shot, because it means that the money goes straight to the manager of the band. This means that the band will never see the money again.

• •

The next thing to happen is the announcement from the side of the stage by the Concert Chairperson Secretary Committee Executive, who will inform the eager crowd that you are about to perform. Again, this is worth listening to. Special attention should be given to the band name, if you are called, say, Dead Slug.

> 'Er... Right then... Er... We've got a good set of lads here tonight... and er... They're only young and they've come a long way to be here tonight... And they've got a lot of expensive equipment up here so I'm sure they'll do their very best... Er... The Dead Slug Show Band... (*Applause*)

N O T E. . . . .
The word 'applause' is used very loosely. The sound is actually very similar to the noise you'd expect if two people hit each other in the face with a piece of wet liver. Which is probably what is happening if the Beef Dinner has already been handed out.

. . . .

The band then take the stage to rapturous silence, and are followed by the trumpet player, who materialized in the dressing room three seconds beforehand. No doubt after finding the lip which had gone.

You should then immediately go into the first number, which will be totally inaudible because of feedback. But who's listening anyway?

CHAPTER NINE

THE RECORDING STUDIO

People who have never been to a Recording Studio believe that it looks like the set-up on the Live Aid video. This is not true. Recording studios only look like that when you are called Quincey Jones, Genesis, or a Charity Record.

NOTE. . . . .
A 'Charity Record' is a record made by a lot of people that you thought died ages ago, or are friends of Slade. Bobby Stallion tends to turn up these records. (The Live Aid record was a fake. Nearly everyone was recognizable.)
. . . .

If you aren't Quincey Jones then when you go to a Recording Studio you will find that it is God-forsaken pit of a hole in the upper floor or basement of a nearly disused factory. This description sounds very similar to the Rehearsal Room. This is because it is usually in the same building or at least in the same high crime rate area as the Rehearsal Room.

Should you be an up and coming band (i.e. skint) and

find that the Recording Studio you are booked into *isn't* a God-forsaken pit of a hole in a high crime rate area, then it is advised that you turn round and go home immediately. This is advisable for two reasons: (1) The charge per hour will be so high you'll only be able to afford the drum track. (2) If the charge per hour isn't extortionate, then it means the Recording Studio is subsidized by the Council and run by a strange person of no fixed sex who watches Channel 4 and 'knows what the kids want'. This is not good, and should be avoided.

Recording Studios always smell of old feet, old cigarettes and old carpets. This is because the room contains all three. It also contains lots of dirty coffee cups and empty take-away food packets but you can't smell them over the pong of feet and cigarettes.

Also, because all the holes in the doors, windows, floor and ceiling have been blocked up to stop the noise getting out, there is very little air getting in. This gives you a pretty good idea of what it is like being trapped in a submarine. Especially a submarine where everyone eats Kentucky Fried Chicken and smokes a lot.

Around the walls of the control room you will see posters, leads, fist marks, leads, headphones and more leads. The posters are usually very strange, the headphones only work on one side until you waggle the cord and hold it in the right position, and the leads belong to something that the studio used to have but sold and got a new one and it might fit something so they haven't thrown it away.

The fist marks belong to the last band that was in there, when the band split because of musical differences. i.e. the guitarist was crap.

In the middle of the control room is a huge mixing desk with a million knobs on it. A lot of these knobs don't do anything. They are there to deter the band from thinking they know what they're doing and interfering, because it all looks very complicated.

The person who works the mixing desk and all the other fiddly knobs is called the Sound Engineer. He is called a lot of other things, depending on the final mix, but the name he answers to is Sound Engineer. Sound Engineers are always very quiet people and have a level of patience that is not human. Most people would commit murder if subjected to the same things that the sound engineer has to put up with. But while all the madness is taking place round him he just sits there fiddling with his knob.

The reason the Sound Engineer can stay so calm when the band insist that the last 16 tracks need doing again, is because (1) He is getting paid; (2) he is probably smashed out of his head.

Next to the control room is a padded cell. This is for putting musicians in, so that everyone can make fun of them without them hearing anything. This is then followed by a comment through the intercom system like, 'Can we just do that once more, Simon?'

MAKING A DEMO TAPE

Making a Demo Tape or record is a very long and very very boring process. A lot of people imagine that making a record is quite exciting, but then some people get off on ice-skating so it's all a matter of taste.

Professional bands who've made records before tend to turn up in the studio in dribs and drabs because they know who is needed in what order and also know that making a record is a very long and very very boring process. However, the amateur band do not know this, and so when they make their first Demo Tape it is quite an event.

The day usually starts with everyone turning up feeling giggly and excited. Except the brass section who might turn up later in the afternoon if you're lucky.

The drummer then sets up his kit and goes Thubum! Thubum! Thubum! Thubum! on the bass drum for about an hour while the recording levels and sound are checked. Then he hits the snare drum and goes Dat! Dat! Dat! Dat! for several more hours. Then he hits the tom-tom and goes Tum! Tum! Tum! Tum! and everyone suddenly realizes that making a record is a very long and very very boring process.

When all the sound levels have been set, the drummer records the basic rhythm for the various songs. This lasts about four hours and 43 takes. You might think it is difficult for a drummer to run through a song without accompaniment. Ordinarily this would be true, but when a drummer plays a song he ignores everyone anyway, so there's little difference. And what with him being stone deaf and everything....

There is also an aid for the drummer called a 'click track'. This is something that clicks at a precise speed so that the drummer has something to keep time with when putting down the initial drum track. What usually happens is that he ignores it because it puts him off. This is very similar to the sound of a metronome coming through the headphones. You would notice the difference immediately if a real metronome came through the headphones because it would smash your brains in.

The most exciting part of the day then takes place. The drummer and all the band pile into the control room and listen to the tape being played back. Everyone stands around and stares in amazement as if they're primitive natives who've never seen a tape recorder before. This would be understandable if they were listening to something more exciting than Fumdum... Dink!...

69

Fumdum... Dink!... Fumdum... Dink!... Roochah!... Roochah!... Fumdum Dink!... etc.

However, they aren't

If the drum track is perfect it is best to throw the drummer out of the recording studio. Otherwise he will spend all day getting in the way and bashing out a rhythm on his legs with the drumsticks, whilst everyone is listening to the guitar solo. This is because the drummer can't hear the guitar solo anyway. He will also claim that the drums are too far back in the mix. But everyone will claim that their instrument is too far back in the mix, so it's best to throw him out whilst the going is good.

The bassist will then do his bit on top of the drum track and insist that it isn't loud enough even when the huge bass cabs in the control room start walking across the floor and the drummer can actually hear it.

The guitarist will then also do his part on the track and insist that he can't hear it. This is common practice. If the guitarist thinks his part sounds right he is either a very professional musician or weird. Or both.

Everyone then stands around in the control room and listens to the tape being played back. This is a great joy to the drummer, the bassist and the guitarist. To everyone else the whole process is becoming very long and very very boring. I told you so.

Keyboards come next. Then the vocals are put down, followed by the brass section who have now turned up if you are lucky. This is very irritating because the brass players have only just got there and think making a record is very exciting, whereas everyone else has now come to the conclusion that it is a very long and very very boring process.

Throughout this whole procedure there is a track called 'guide vocals'. This is in fact a genuine recording of the singer that is put down early on, so that the other instrumentalists have something to work against. The lead singer then spends the whole day explaining to friends and relatives who drop into the studios that they are only 'guide vocals'. This is understandable when you realize the fine distinction between the 'guide vocals' and the final take. The 'guide vocals' sound bloody awful. But then sometimes they both do.

When all the tracks have been done and everyone is feeling faint, sick and very tired because of lack of food and oxygen, someone then says, 'You know what would sound *really* good?'

The rest of the band will then listen while this person suggests rewriting the whole song and the Sound Engineer doesn't even flinch as he sits there fiddling with his knob. Then everyone decides that rewriting the song isn't such a good idea after all and someone will be sent out for food. Unfortunately, they will find that it is now 7.00 p.m. and they are in a high crime rate industrial area, so there aren't any shops open except the Off Licence. This explains why the person sent out for food invariably comes back with four cans of lager, three Bounties, five Kit-Kats and 18 packets of crisps.

The person who has been sent for food will then find that they have an additional problem. They can't get through the severely bolted 10-foot thick padded door, back into the studios, because it is locked and no one on the other side can hear. If there is an intercom system it will be just as he gets to the door that the whole band will decide to listen to the tape all the way through at full volume.

An hour later someone will wonder if maybe the person sent for food is outside the door and go looking for him. There will then be a light-hearted exchange of banter as he enters the control room and throws crisps at everyone. Then he will insist on hearing the tape all the way through at full volume because he missed it.

MIXING

T he mixing of the final recording usually takes place a day or two after the recording session. This gives the band a chance to eat properly and breathe real air before locking themselves in the studio again and having a good argument. The less members of the band there are at the Mixing Session, the better. The tracks won't sound any better but there will be less arguing, especially from the drummer who can't hear anything anyway.

The idea of a Mixing Session is to set the individual levels of the independent tracks so that when the full tape is played back it will sound brilliant. Unfortunately there has to be something brilliant there in the first place. This can be a bit disappointing to the band when the Sound Engineer can't give them a Number One single from a pile of junk.

NOTE. . . . .

A lot of Number One singles are a pile of junk. This is not the Sound Engineer's fault. He was probably smashed out of his head anyway. He probably had to be.

. . . .

During the mix there is a common phenomenon called 'Hearing Blindness'. This is caused by hearing the same song so many times that you are sick to death of it. Then, just as the whole song is about to be dumped to tape, the bassist will come back from the shop clutching three Mars Bars and a Bounty and point out that there is no bass drum on the track. Everyone will then go, 'Bloody hell, he's right!' and the mixing will start all over again.

Hearing Blindness also causes you to keep turning one part higher and higher until you can't hear anything else, then the bass is turned up, then the drums are turned up, then the vocals are turned up. Then everyone realizes that they can't hear each other shouting across the mixing desk and the whole thing is turned down again.

THE FINAL MIX

T he Final Mix is the state of the recording when everyone was so sick of it that they gave up. Unfortunately, the Final Mix sounds pretty good on the £2000 super-deluxe speakers in the studio. You can tell

73

that it sounds good because everyone looks at each other and says 'Yeah'. This is a sure sign that everyone is happy.

It is only when you get home and play the cassette tape on your £15 Hong Kong sound centre that you realize it is a pile of junk.

In fact one of the biggest break-throughs you will make is when you slip a Demo Tape into your cassette deck and play it without someone screwing up their face and saying 'What's *that?*'

It isn't so bad if they say 'What's *that?*', while pointing to your tariburgle, because I don't know what one is either and would probably do the same. However, when they are obviously referring to your Demo Tape it can be quite hurtful.

The opposite of this reaction occurs when someone doesn't know what a Demo Tape really is and thinks that just because you've been in a recording studio, you must be famous. They go round telling people that they know you and that you will be on *TOTP*'s and a millionaire in two weeks, and they keep turning up on your door step. This is wonderful if they are a good-looking member of the opposite sex, but this is rarely the case. The best thing to do is take them quietly to one side and tell them as diplomatically and kindly as you can, to piss off.

After about two hours of playing your Demo Tape non-stop you will find yourself looking in a mirror and regarding a huge spot on your face. This is caused by eating Mars Bars, Kit-Kats and Bounties all day. This is not normally serious unless the band's photo session is due to take place the following day. Which, invariably, it is.

CHAPTER TEN

THE PHOTO SESSION

For most amateur bands the Photo Session is nothing more than an excuse for everyone to pose in stupid clothes with stupid expressions on their faces. The reason they do this is because all the pictures they've ever seen of professional bands show them standing around in stupid clothes with stupid expressions on their faces, so they feel that they should do the same.

The photos themselves are usually taken by a friend of the brother-in-law of the guitarist, who took someone's wedding photos so he must be pretty good. The quote, 'So he must be pretty good,' usually comes from the guitarist rather than the poor souls who had the most memorable day of their lives ruined by a clod of a photographer.

What usually happens is that the band turn up at some exotic outside location and ponce about while the photographer does complicated things with his camera. It appears that the photographer is fiddling with lenses and light settings, but what he's really doing is trying to remember which bit makes the shutter go up and down (or whatever it does), in the hope that this precaution will stop the band hitting him like the young couple did the week before.

An 'exotic outside location', for some strange reason, turns out to be the inside of a disused factory or the shell of a partly demolished house. Most bands seem to think that if they are seen hanging around the door frame of a nearly collapsed brick terraced house, it will give them some sort of 'street cred'. This same thinking accounts for the many shots of bands:

1. Sitting on walls with a factory behind them.
2. All looking through the window of a bombed out terraced house.
3. All standing on a pile of bricks at a demolition site.
4. All posing around the inside of a disused factory so that the black and white photos will look 'dead moody'.
5. All frantically trying to look mean, which usually results in them all looking pretty stupid.

There are also several snags about posing in a factory or on a demolition site. The first one being that there is no mirror for everyone to look at in order to confirm that they look as cool/street-wise/macho, as they think they look. The first person to notice this is the lead singer because the singer is even more vain than the guitarist. Also, there is the added complication of the hats and strange clothes. The hats and strange clothes were brought by one of the band in the hope that if everyone dressed up, they would look cool/street-wise/bloody silly. So the result is that each member of the band wears whatever they think is right and then asks the other members of the band how it looks. This means that the most unpopular member of the band ends up with a silly purple felt hat, with the assurance that it looks terrific.

NOTE. . . . .
Prince sometimes wears a silly purple felt hat.
This is because no one in the band likes him.
. . . .

Another snag with taking band photographs outdoors is the people who keep passing by and stopping to have a look. It is about now that you suddenly realize you are hanging around a demolished brick terraced house, wearing a purple hat, fake leopard skin trousers and trying to look mean. Five seconds after this you begin to feel very silly indeed and pray that the group of skinheads

CLICK!

you saw earlier, don't turn up unexpectedly. This dread is soon forgotten by the embarrassment of seeing a bus queue forming on the other side of the road and people in office blocks staring out of the window at you.

This is why, out of the eight rolls of film taken by the friend of the brother-in-law of the guitarist, only two photos are suitable. This is because they are the only ones where everyone is looking in the right direction, and don't have a piece of pipe, lamp post, or cooling tower sticking out of their head. Though in some cases the addition of a piece of scaffolding sticking out of someone's head can be quite an improvement, and for the photographer it's a relief that anything came out at all.

You will notice as you look through the photos that the lead singer has somehow always managed to appear in front of everyone else. Even though he was supposed to be at the back somewhere. This is because he thinks it is *his* band and doesn't see why the rest of the band should be in the photo anyway. This view can sometimes be detected when the lead singer suggests taking a few shots of him standing by himself, 'Just to finish off this roll of film.' Unless you stop him quickly he will take up all the film.

This doesn't really matter, because the lead singer will eventually go to a professional to get some pretentious photos taken anyway. This has many advantages for the lead singer because:

1. Those other people (the band) can't get in the way when he gets his pose right.
2. The pictures of his face are three times bigger than on a group photo.
3. He can wear the stupid leotard top that all the band wet themselves over when he wore it last time.
4. No one in the band will know that he's ordered 200 copies of the best photo.

The other way of doing band photos is to go to a professional. By 'professional' I mean someone who charges you so much money you feel sick in the stomach. This is the best way to make a band feel that the photos are really good, even though they aren't. This sort of hassle can be overcome by going to Pete's Photo Emporium in Chester, where you will receive a friendly and professional service at very reasonable prices. 'Yes, folks, Pete's Photo Emporium is the place to be for quality service.'...(Thank you. No, cash is fine.)

Going to a professional photographer is a very interesting experience. Various questions immediately spring to mind when you enter the premises.

Various Questions

1. Do people who come to have their photograph taken actually read the boring magazines on the table?
2. Why does everyone in the photos on the wall look like Bobby Stallion?
3. Why do they have a coffee percolator but no cups, coffee, milk or sugar?
4. In the photo room itself, what is that huge roll of white paper hanging from the ceiling for?
5. Whose footprints are those on that huge roll of white paper hanging from the ceiling?
6. Why is the guitarist's nose only an inch away from a black and white photo on the other side of the room?
7. Why are the photographer's staff pretending they are busy when they obviously aren't?

These questions are never answered. Or if they are, you're too busy posing to hear the answers.

The lead singer will have brought his assistant with him. The 'assistant' is a friend of someone who knows the guitarist's brother, who does a make-up course in the evenings. It will be her job to use her vast make-up skills to cover up the spot on the lead singer's nose. That's the general idea, but once the lead singer gets in front of a mirror there's no turning back. There will be just a little foundation to give a better complexion, a teeny touch of eyeliner to make the eyes slightly fuller, a dab – just a dab, mind you – of lipstick so that his features will show up better under the lights. And on and on and on. The result looks like something from KISS. In fact it was this very process that give KISS their image. They were originally trying to look like Keith Richards.

When everyone has catered to their vanity and is ready to have their photo taken the photographer will spend half an hour messing about with the huge roll of white paper hanging from the ceiling. From the state of it, it can only be assumed that he is trying to find a set of footprints that match the band's.

The photographer will then mess about with an umbrella, a plastic plant, a lamp, and the bass player because he's quite cute.

Then the whole band will stand on the white piece of paper looking very stupid and the photographer will suggest that the drummer takes his finger out of his nose, the lead singer should move a yard backwards so that he is part of the band, and is it really necessary for the guitarist to hold his hand like that?

THEN everyone will settle down and the photographer will step back and in the astounding silence that follows there will be a slight... nothing. But it's all OK. just a bad lead to the flash and are we ready?... Ready?... Nothing.

There then follows a half-hour interval while the photographer tries to get the flash working, which is, 'Very expensive and the best in the world and Lord

Lichfield uses one,' and any other lie he can think of while trying to get the flash going.

THEN he will finally get everything working and take a lot of photos of the band looking mean, but not half as many as the moody lighting shots, the one where the lead singer sits on the guitarist's shoulders, the ones of the drummer playing drums on the bassist's chest, the ones of the band hiding behind the plastic plant and the ones of the whole band in tier formation with the singer and guitarist kneeling at the front and everyone else standing at the back as if they were a six-a-side football team that had just won something.

THEN the photographer says something that he heard in a film once and thinks is really clever, like 'It's in the can,' and everyone goes home.

THEN three days later you all look at the photos and realize that three quarters of them are of the band hiding behind a plastic plant in moody lighting, or posing like a six-a-side football team. The one single shot of everyone looking human is the final choice and only cost you fifty quid.

All this agony could have been prevented if you'd only gone to Pete's Photo Emporium. (Thank you. No, cash is fine.)

Previously Unknown Moments in History: No 6
GLENN MILLER: The violinists' coach has broken down, so if the Saxes could cover their part just for tonight...

CHAPTER ELEVEN

THE VAN

The Van is that huge mess of a thing that chokes and splutters its way up and down the country with the Roadie in it. The choking and spluttering is the noise coming from the Roadie. When the Roadie isn't talking about sex or high impedance he will be talking about the Van. This is because it keeps breaking down and needs, taxing, new tyres, new gears, new spare tyre, new cylinder head, new everything else. This is quite common. There is not a Band's Van in the world that has a full set of treaded tyres, a spare wheel, *and* a jack.

If you find that your Band's Van has a spare wheel *and* a jack it is best to abandon it quickly because it is obviously stolen.

At the back of a standard Band's Van there should be a bracket which has been badly welded to the back doors. This is for clamping a huge padlock to, so that people won't break into the Van, yet again. The reason it is so badly welded is because every time someone forgets the key, the bracket has to be sawn through and a new one fitted. This goes on for as long as there is some door left to weld a bracket to. Or until someone steals the Van.

On long journeys in the Van you will notice something going Shhhhh-crackle-crackle-mumble-Shhhhh. This is the radio. It can never be heard over the noise of the engine and sometimes even sounds the same when the engine isn't running. Films of Buddy Holly and people like that, which show them all listening to their latest hit as they travel to the next concert in the Van, are a figment of the

Producer's imagination. After an hour in a Band's Van you couldn't hear Concorde if it landed on your head, let alone a crackly radio.

The radio is usually situated next to the thing that blows cold air on to your feet for three hours in winter. This is the Heater. The Heater is called a Heater because ... because everything needs to be called something. Otherwise the world would be full of 'whatsits' and 'thingies'. The Heater doesn't actually heat anything so it is presumed that its main purpose is to freeze the lower half of the band for three hours, so that they don't think about sex so much. The effect is very similar to swimming in the sea. This doesn't bother the female members of the band unless they are wearing a thin T-shirt, but the male members will complain of stomach-ache. This is because that's where their testicles are hiding.

If you are lucky/unlucky enough to have a Van with a long wheel base, you may find that it has two rows of seats. This is so that *all* the band can travel to the next concert in the same Van and *all* arrive deaf, aching, needing a piss, and frozen solid from the waist down.

The seats are very often aeroplane seats, cinema seats, or any other seats that were easy to steal at the time. Which is how they appeared in the back of the Van in the first place. This is the reason why they are not always bolted down and fly over backwards when the Roadie does a racing start at the traffic lights. The Roadie doing a racing start at the traffic lights is why the Van has bald tyres. The Van having bald tyres is why you were pulled over by the police. The Roadie telling the policeman to bugger off is why... etc... etc... The fact that you are in Turkey is why you are all going to be hanged tomorrow morning.

But back to the seats.

The seats in the second row are very like any other

seats, except they are too close together, wobble, fall over backwards and are covered in crumbs. The crumbs are left there by the Crumb Fairy.

Facts about The Crumb Fairy

1. The Crumb Fairy leaves bits of crisps in every available seat in the van.
2. The Crumb Fairy seems to follow the Roadie everywhere.
3. The mess on the floor of the van/rehearsal room/ recording studio, is the work of the Crumb Fairy.

This should not be confused with the sinister activity of the Empty Kentucky Fried Chicken Box Fairy, or even the Empty Crisp Packet Fairy, who are all equally active in the van/rehearsal room/recording studio etc. And all this has nothing at all to do with the Clap Fairy, which is a whole different story. Interestingly enough, the Clap Fairy also seems to follow the Roadie everywhere.

But back to the Van. The Van has the uncanny ability to break down just when you are in the most hostile God-forsaken, cold, wet hell-hole in the world. Which oddly enough is a small road in Scotland somewhere between Fort William and Glasgow. Or anywhere near Birmingham.

When the Van breaks down it is the Roadie's job to get out and lift the bonnet. This can be quite tricky because there's usually a mile of gaffer tape holding it down ever since it flew off on the M5 and everyone spent half an hour looking for it. But when the Roadie does finally lift the bonnet and everyone has (a) got out and had a piss, (b) stood around bobbing from foot to foot and mentioning how cold it is, (c) looked under the bonnet and said 'What's wrong, then?' (d) climbed back into the Van, it can

84

then be concluded that the Roadie doesn't know a great deal about engines. In fact, after a few of these episodes it becomes fairly obvious that the only knowledge the Roadie has of car maintenance, comes from watching a Pretty Polly stockings advert. Also, as it's unlikely that the fan belt is at fault anyway, and as the Roadie doesn't wear stockings (all the time), he is not going to be a great deal of help. Three seconds after this conclusion is reached everyone then finds out that there isn't anyone in the band who is a member of the AA or the RAC.

For some strange reason there is always at least one person in the band who thinks pushing a fully loaded transit van in the middle of the night is a real hoot. Whether this is some form of hysteria or not, is unknown, but the fact that everyone else in the band wants to beat his brains in is a fact.

After what seems days, you will arrive at a garage. But I don't know anything about garages so I'll talk about something else.

SOMETHING ELSE

Unanswered questions of the Universe

1. Why are so many joggers still alive when they run full tilt up the wrong side of the road in the middle of the night?
2. Why do hedgehogs get run over by lorries when all they're doing is running full tilt up the wrong side of road in the middle of the night?
3. If eating all that spinach had *really* made you grow up to be like Popeye, would your parents have been happy when you turned into a squint-eyed, ham-armed, bow-legged sailor?

CHAPTER TWELVE

FLY-POSTING, ETC.

There are two methods most commonly used by bands when they wish to inform the public that they will be giving a performance in the near future. The first is used by bands who are signed up and get lots of money from a record company. This involves putting an advert in a newspaper or music magazine, which everyone ignores. The other method, employed by bands who haven't got a record deal or any money, is to put up posters all over town, which everyone then ignores.

The idea behind Fly-Posting is to vandalize any public building not in use – any telephone box, any bus stop and any old aged pensioners who aren't walking fast enough when you pass them with a wadge of posters and a bucket of splodge.

This will ensure that at least nine out of ten people who catch a bus, use a public building, or know an old aged pensioner will become aware of a badly photocopied poster staring them in the face. The fact that it can't be read and makes little sense is usually not enough to dissuade a band that their efforts are reaping tremendous rewards. Even when they print a red poster on a green

background or a green poster on a red background and expect you to be able to read it as you flash past on the bus or are standing next to it in orange street lighting. But, well, it keeps them happy.

The other disadvantage of Fly-Posting the whole town is that there is a fair chance before you even perform, the band will (a) split up, (b) change their name, (c) kick you out, (d) change the venue.

This is not quite as distressing as when the police turn up at the gig and would like to have a quiet word with you about defacing public property.

And, funnily enough, all this is not as distressing as being shot or losing a leg or being set on fire.

THE GUEST LIST

The Guest List is probably the best way of losing friends, assuming that you still have any. This is

87

because everyone seems to assume they should get into the gig for nothing, and usually on the flimsiest of reasons. Reasons like... they're in the band.

The best way of overcoming this problem is to tell everyone that you will put their name on the Guest List, but don't actually bother. This means that a lot people turn up and rather than go away again they stump up the money. You can then shrug your shoulders and say, 'Well, I put it on the list.' The little known saxophonist Cool Drool used to do this quite often, until he was found out and dropped from the band. Or, rather, from the building the band were playing in.

Sometimes the management of various clubs don't allow Guest Lists because they don't like the idea of people getting in for free. This accounts for a great many pub bands that turn up with 18 roadies, half of which are female and don't even have a black T-shirt or a bundle of keys.

The bouncer on the door will sometimes let you in even if your name isn't on the list, because he can't read. This is also the same reason he *won't* let you in when it *is* on the list.

GAFFER TAPE

A lot of people think that bands are held together by mutual respect and complementary musical creativity, whereas most bands are held together with Gaffer Tape. For anyone who has never come across this incredibly useful stuff, it is a type of tape made from old rags and concrete which can hold an elephant down, lift a Jumbo jet up, and keep the Roadie's flies closed.

When the nuclear holocaust comes there will only be two things still surviving on Earth. Cockroaches and Gaffer Tape.

Other uses of Gaffer Tape are:
1. Fastening wires to the stage.
2. Fastening wires to the walls.
3. Fastening wires to the wires.
4. Fastening bits back on to the drum kit.
5. Fastening bits back on to the Roadie.
6. Holding your trousers up.
7. Holding the cymbal case shut.
8. Ripping the wallpaper off the wall when you come to take the wires down again.
9. Ripping the tiles off the floor when you come to take the wires up again.
10. Putting over people's mouths when you commit a bank robbery.
11. Mending the van.
12. Safe sex.

The story of Gaffer Tape is an interesting one. Many years ago there was a King who had a servant who did something really good. I can't remember what it was that he did, but anyway. 'That's dead good,' said the King. 'How would you like your dosh?' And the servant said, 'King,' he said. 'If you put two grains of rice on the first square of a chess board and then double that number on the next square until all the chess board is filled, I will accept that as my payment.' And the King put his head in his hands and looked at the servant and said, 'What's a chess board, then?' because no one had invented it yet. And the servant didn't know either so the King had the servant taken out and shot. Then the King became very bored and invented some very strong tape and named it after the servant who'd just been shot. Wilfred Smith.

Then he changed his mind and called it Gaffer Tape instead.

And that's why we have Gaffer Tape today.

CHAPTER THIRTEEN

THE BLUES

The Blues should have a section all of its own. Some people think that it should have a planet of its own, but I quite like the Blues.

The Blues was invented by black people so that white guitarists would feel inadequate and take drugs. One of the most successful at this was a white guitarist called Blind Lemon Arkwright, who was pretty rubbishy at the Blues, but, boy, could he take drugs. In fact it was because of his drug taking that his hit song 'Got a good woman on my mind' was banned in six countries when he insisted on singing 'Got a good woman on my head', though it's believed he couldn't tell the difference. And anyway, when you come down to it, what is a good woman?

The most popular form of Blues is twelve-bar Blues. There are a lot of eight-bar blues around but that's just because the guitarist is trying so hard he's lost count.

Should you be intelligent enough to understand the many guitar tutors around, you will eventually come across the various chord charts. After a few moments glancing at the guitar tutor, at least three questions will immediately spring to mind.

1. Do I really want to play guitar that badly?
2. Why does the man in the black and white picture look so smug?
3. Is that man in the picture the same man with the stupid shirt and haircut who does those appalling Open

University programmes on a Sunday morning when I've got a hangover and just switched on the television because I haven't got anything more interesting to do with my life than watch some git with a paisley shirt tell me about Isosceles Progressions? Or not?

Anyway, if you do manage to make sense of the book, you will eventually be introduced to the chord sequence which makes up a standard twelve-bar Blues.

The form that the Blues takes is I,I,I,I7, IV,IV,I,I, V,IV,I,V, which comes to two million thousand and five if you're a Roman. However, if you aren't a Roman then it's quite easy to see the form that the Blues takes. Apparently.

The 7 in the fourth bar indicates that there is a flattened seventh, whereas the 'I' in the first bar signifies

91

that it's the beginning of the song, as in 'I woke up this morning'. The IV signifies that it is the chord based on the fourth note of the root chord and the V in the last set of four bars signifies that you should have reached the part of the verse where you throw back your head and sing 'You don't groan when we make love no more.' This is different to the last 'V' where you are supposed to say something like 'Tell me baby... tell me.'. But don't worry too much about these rules as they're probably all wrong anyway.

A popular addition to playing the guitar is to attempt to play harmonica at the same time. This is not easy to do, as was illustrated by Dylan, though he was still pretty good for a rabbit.

The reason that the harmonica is so difficult to play is that it takes you most of your life to find out what key it's supposed to be in. Then you only have a few years to practise before you die.

Naturally enough, there is a good explanation for the fact that you play a G harmonica when you want to play against a Blues in A. It's all to do with flattened thirds and sevenths, but then what isn't?... and why not? The only complication to this is that you spend six notes sucking in for every one you blow out. This can result in a rather thin tone, or, more usually, death. This is, of course, another reason it is called the Blues, indicating the colour of a harmonica player's face after a solo.

Interestingly enough, the playing of harmonica in G against a Blues in A was discovered quite accidentally by a salesman from Detroit called Dyslexic Willie Arkwright, who became famous for the song 'I Wok up Tihs Minring Blues'.

The construction of the words used in Blues also follows a particular pattern. This pattern has been handed down from generation to generation and is quite straightforward.

92

Part One: A statement designed to arouse sympathy.
Part Two: The same statement with 'I said' put on the front.
Part Three: The punch line, verifying the circumstances or sentiments expressed in Parts One and Two.
For example:
I woke up this morning with them Blues on my mind. I said... I woke up this morning with them Blues on my mind.
My legs done dropped off and I think I'm going blind.

This poetic form can also be used to create a Blues out of just about anything.

For example:
I eat my peas with butter babe, I've done it all my life.
Yeah I said... I eat my peas with butter babe, I've gone done it all my life.
It sure make them peas taste funny babe, but it keeps them on the knife. (SPOKEN ADLIB: We're talking peas babe... tell me 'bout it.)

That old Duke of York's a dude babe, got ten thousand men yeah.
I said... That old Duke of York's a dude babe, got ten thousand men.
Done march them up the hill now, then he march them down again. (SPOKEN ADLIB: They was just walking babe... like they was just walking.)

It is because it is so easy to make up words for the Blues that many of them go on for days at a time, until either all the audience go home or the band drop dead. Which sometimes is no bad thing.

93

CHAPTER FOURTEEN

FAME

If you work hard and have a great deal of talent, then after a few years and a lot of struggle sod all will happen. However, if you're one of those lucky people who is just the same as everyone else but happened to be in the right place at the right time, you may find that you become famous.

Should you actually become famous, you will find several things happen to you.

1. All your friends will start acting funny and talk to you as if you've got something hanging from your nose.
2. You will remember in graphic detail the drunken night you spent with the exotic dancer, the bondage chains and the banana and hope that she doesn't remember you equally as well when she sees your picture in the paper.
3. People you have never met will talk to you in the hope that they are seen talking to you.
4. The British press will crucify you.
5. A totally untrue fabricated story will appear in the *Sun* about you, an exotic dancer, and a banana.

Fame is not necessarily a good thing. All that happens is that you get to meet all the people you've ever admired. Get picked up by beautiful people of the opposite sex and earn lots of money. Then there's all that bind about getting into nightclubs for free and being given the best seat in the restaurant so that the manager can creep round you all night. So it's pretty awful really.

There are also the spin-off products of being famous. For instance, just how many times can you seriously answer questions about the stupid name of the band you made up one night? And who gives a toss what colour socks you wear and what you sleep in? And just because Jim Fixed it you have to be really nice to some little girl who can't sing. And who in their right mind wants to live in London anyway and be seen at Stringfellows just because someone from *East Enders* goes there to be photographed every five minutes? That's assuming, of course, that Oliver Reed isn't there dropping his trousers at the time or half the members of the latest up-and-coming band aren't laughing hysterically knowing full well that the man with six cameras round his neck pointing one at them isn't just a bouncer with a hobby?

But, anyway, where was I?

Unless you move to America, or somewhere where they actually like people with money, you will then be systematically and mercilessly held up for ridicule by the very same tabloid newspapers who were holding a competition to give away a signed copy of your knickers only two months before. Unfortunately, the same people who read these papers are the ones who believed them in the first place and made you famous. They will, sadly, also believe everything they now read and decide to take down your poster from their bedroom wall and never eat bananas again. So you've blown it, mate.

This means that you may suddenly disappear into obscurity and never be seen again, much to the delight of the people who used to be your friends before you became such a big headed git. I mean, what ever happened to Catcha Goolie? What happened to Zig Zig Spitball? Would you recognize any members of the Wombles and would you still want to hit them even now?

Come to think of it, maybe it's just as well some people do sink into obscurity never to be seen again.

And Finally

1. A G string in the hand is worth the effort.
2. Roadies can't help it. They were born that way.
3. The last words of General Wayne Jones, part-time drummer and the man responsible for accidentally setting off the nuclear attack on Russia, were, 'I weren't doing anything.'